30X(4/05)4/11

D0461544

LAST

The Discovery Books are prepared
under the educational supervision of
Mary C. Austin, Ed.D.
Professor of Education
University of Hawaii
Honolulu

A DISCOVERY BOOK

GARRARD PUBLISHING COMPANY
CHAMPAIGN, ILLINOIS

Mary McLeod Bethune
Teacher with a Dream

by LaVere Anderson
illustrated by William Hutchinson

Library of Congress Cataloging in Publication Data

Anderson, LaVere.
    Mary McLeod Bethune, teacher with a dream.

    (A Discovery book)
    SUMMARY: A biography of the black woman who spent
her life educating and working to earn basic human rights
for her people.

    1. Bethune, Mary Jane McLeod, 1875-1955. [1. Bethune,
Mary Jane McLeod, 1875-1955. 2. Teachers. 3. Negroes
—Biography] I. Hutchinson, William M. II. Title.

LA2317.B39A62   370'.92'4 [B] [92]   75-25765
ISBN 0-8116-6321-3

Contents

Chapter *1*

Cabin in the Cotton

Mary Jane McLeod ran from the cabin into the front yard. Granny Sophia sat rocking in her chair under a big oak tree. "Child, where are you going all dressed up so clean and pretty?" granny asked. "My, you smell like soap and sunshine."

"I'm going with mama to take Mrs. Wilson's wash home," six-year-old Mary said. "Mama says the Wilson children have a new playhouse that is just like a real little house! I'm going to see it."

"You remember to act like a lady in that little house," granny said. "Don't let those white children think your mama didn't raise you right."

Just then Mary's mother came from the cabin. She carried a basket of freshly washed clothes on her head.

They told granny good-bye and started down the dusty country road. Soon they passed a cotton field. Several of Mary's brothers and sisters were picking cotton. Mary shouted and waved to them.

"I'm glad you let me come with you today, mama," Mary said. "I don't like to pick cotton. It is hard work."

Mrs. McLeod smiled. "Yes, it is. But this is our own cotton we are picking. We are working for ourselves. We are not working for a white master, as we did in slave days."

Mary had heard the story about slavery

many times. Her granny had been a slave. So had Mary's parents, Sam and Patsy McLeod, and their older children. Some of those children had been taken from them and sold to other masters. Then the Civil War had freed the slaves. Mary had been born ten years after the war, on July 10, 1875.

"Praise the Lord, you were born free!" Granny often told Mary.

After the war both Mary's mother and father had worked for their old masters and saved their pay. In time they saved enough to buy a little cotton farm in Mayesville, South Carolina. They were so proud of the farm. But some years their crops were poor! It was hard to make the money they needed to raise their many children. So Mrs. McLeod earned extra money washing clothes for white families.

Mrs. McLeod and Mary turned in at the Wilsons' gate. Mary stopped at the playhouse in the yard. When she peeked through the open door, she saw one of the Wilson girls.

"Do you want to see my house, Mary Jane?" the girl asked.

Mary stepped inside. She looked around with delight. There were real little chairs and tables. There were tiny dishes on the tables and a sewing basket. There was even a book. Mary had never held a book. She picked it up carefully.

"Mary Jane, put that book down!" the girl ordered.

"I wasn't going to hurt it," Mary said.

"You can't read. Put it down. Come here, and I'll show you some pictures in this other book."

Mary crossed the room and looked at the pictures. They were of many strange

animals. Mary pointed to one of them. "What is that, miss?"

"An elephant," the girl said. She read from the book: "Many elephants live in Africa."

Africa! "Why, I know about Africa!" Mary thought. Granny was always telling stories about it. She said that Africa was the real home of black people. White men had gone there and brought blacks across the ocean to be slaves. Granny said that Mary's great-grandfather had been a prince there.

"Oh, I'd like to read what that book says about Africa!" Mary exclaimed.

"Don't be silly, Mary Jane." The girl's voice was sharp. "*You* can't read. Black children never read."

From the yard Mary's mother called to her.

"Good-bye, miss." Mary ran out of the

playhouse. She was very glad to get away from the girl. Why was it silly to want to read?

On the way home they went by Eli Cooper's place. He was a cotton dealer who bought all of the crops grown by the Mayesville farmers.

"There's your papa," Mrs. McLeod said to Mary. "He is selling the cotton we picked yesterday."

"Let's go watch, mama," Mary said.

They watched the white dealer weigh the cotton.

"You have 250 pounds, Sam," he said.

Mr. McLeod looked surprised. "Seems like it should weigh more, Mr. Cooper. It made such a load that Old Bush had trouble pulling the wagon." Old Bush was the McLeods' bushy-tailed mule.

"The scales say 250 pounds," the dealer said. "Look for yourself."

Quick anger rose in Mary. Eli Cooper knew papa couldn't read the numbers on the scales. Neither could mama.

Back on the road, Mary asked her mother, "How do we know that Mr. Cooper didn't cheat us?"

"We don't. We have to trust him."

"Humph!" Mary said to herself. If she could read words and learn numbers, she would know *just* how much papa's cotton weighed. Then nobody could cheat him. She could read about Africa too. And she could borrow the preacher's Bible and read Bible stories to Granny Sophia. Granny loved hearing the preacher read at church.

"Mama," Mary said, "I want to learn to read."

"Child, you can't. None of us know how. Before the war it was against the law to teach Negroes to read. You know there's no school here for black children."

"But I was born free," Mary thought. "It's not fair that I can't learn just as white children do."

The dust was hot under her bare feet. She kicked at it angrily. "I *will* learn," she told herself. But how?

She began to pray. "Oh please, God, have somebody teach me to read."

Chapter 2

Five Miles to School

A busy year passed for Mary and her family. In the spring they planted cotton. All summer they weeded the long rows of plants. Now it was picking time again.

Up and down the rows Mary went. Her fingers were quick as she gathered the soft, white balls and dropped them into a bag. The bag was growing heavy. Mary's heart was heavy too. She remembered last picking time and her visit to the playhouse. She remembered the words, "You can't read."

"I'm a year older," Mary thought, "and nothing has changed."

"Mary Jane, come here," her mother called.

Mary looked across the field. She saw a pretty, black woman with her mother. Mary ran to them.

"I am Miss Emma Wilson," the woman told Mary.

Miss? Mary could not remember ever hearing a black person called "Miss," or "Mrs.," or "Mr." before. Blacks were just called by their first names, as though they had no others. Yet this black lady had said she was *Miss* Emma Wilson. It sounded nice to Mary's ears. "When I grow up, I am going to be *Miss* Mary McLeod," she told herself.

"Miss Emma teaches school," Mary's

mother explained. "She was sent here by the Presbyterian Church. The church has a Board of Missions for Freedmen. It sends teachers to places where there are no schools for freed slaves. Miss Emma is starting a school here."

"And I have room for another pupil," Miss Emma said, smiling.

"Do you still want to learn to read, Mary Jane?" Mrs. McLeod asked.

Did she! "Yes, mama!" Mary cried.

A few days later Mary started down the road to Mayesville. It was five miles to the school. She thought she looked nice. Mama had washed her red dress carefully. Papa had bought her some new shoes and a shiny, tin lunch pail. She was ready for school!

Yet when she reached the one-room schoolhouse, Mary felt suddenly afraid. "I won't know how to act," she thought.

Then she saw Miss Emma standing at the door. The teacher smiled and held out her hands to Mary. In a gentle voice she said, "Come in, Mary Jane. We have been expecting you. I hope you will be happy with us."

Mary forgot she was afraid. "Oh, I will be!" she cried.

So Mary's schooling began. To her, the school looked wonderful. Yet it was really small and poor.

There were no desks. The children had to sit on wooden benches. They had few books and no pencils or paper. She wrote on a slate with chalk. The little wood stove often smoked as it warmed the room. Sometimes the smoke was so thick that Mary could hardly see the letters on her slate.

Even so the school was a happy place. Mary soon learned to read, write, and to

do arithmetic. Since she was bright, she learned quickly. She loved school.

She did not mind the five-mile walk each way. In winter it was often dark before she reached the cabin. At once her brothers and sisters would crowd around her. "Tell us what you learned today," they begged.

"After supper," Mary promised.

As soon as Mary could read, she began to teach the other children.

One night she came home, her eyes shining. She laid a small black book on her grandmother's lap.

"The Mission Board sent a box of Bibles to our school," Mary said. "Miss Emma gave me one, so I could read to you."

After supper the McLeods listened while Mary read. It was a great night in their lives. Tears ran down Granny Sophia's old cheeks. "Praise the Lord," she said. "Our Mary Jane can read the Good Book."

When it was cotton-picking time again, Mary went with her father to take a load to Eli Cooper's.

The dealer weighed the cotton.

"You have 280 pounds, Sam," he said.

Mary had been looking at the scales. "Isn't it 480 pounds?" she asked.

The dealer looked at the scales again. He pretended to be surprised. "It *is* 480 pounds. Why, Mary, you're smart! Now you are learning something!"

Mary smiled to herself. She knew that Eli Cooper was learning something too. He was learning that he could not cheat her father anymore.

Other poor farmers, both black and white, heard the story. They asked Mary to help them. Like Sam McLeod, they had had no schooling. Mary helped them to figure the weight of their cotton. She told them how much money they owed to the storekeepers.

"We are lucky to have Mary Jane," the farmers told Mary's parents.

After three years Mary graduated from Miss Emma's school. "You are ready now to go away to a school for older girls, Mary Jane," the teacher said.

At home Mary told her parents, "I want to go on learning. I want to be just like Miss Emma."

Her father said, "I will help you. I will give you some money from next year's cotton crop."

Spring came. The McLeods went to the field to plant their new crop. Mary's brother, William, hitched Old Bush to the plow. But the tired, old mule could not pull it through the hard earth. His head hung low. His breath came fast.

Then he fell to the ground. Mr. McLeod ran his hand over Old Bush's neck.

"Mule's dead," he said.

"No!" Mary cried. She knelt down and patted her old friend's quiet head. Then another thought struck her. Without a mule, they could not plow. No plowing meant no cotton. No cotton meant no school. She began to sob into Old Bush's mane.

Young William picked up the straps of the plow and put them over his own thin shoulders. Then he pulled as hard as he could.

Suddenly Mary felt ashamed. How could she cry for herself when the family was in trouble? She jumped up and ran to the plow. She pushed it as William pulled. She was big and strong for her age, and she could push hard. Slowly the heavy plow began to move.

Chapter 3

Mary Gets Her Chance

"Mary Jane, don't pick so fast," Mary's little sister Hattie said. "You always pick more cotton than I do."

Mary smiled and said, "Don't worry, Hattie. When you are twelve, like me, you'll pick fast too."

A hot September sun shone down on the working family. This year's crop was small. Without Old Bush, the McLeods had not been able to plow all their land. "There will be no money for school," Mary thought sadly. "There will not even be enough to buy another mule."

Just then a happy voice shouted, "Good news!"

Mary saw Miss Emma coming up the road. The teacher was waving a piece of paper. The McLeods hurried to meet her.

It *was* good news. Miss Emma had been waving a letter from Miss Mary Chrissman, a white teacher in Colorado.

"Miss Chrissman believes in freedom and schooling for all black people," Miss Emma told the McLeods. "She is poor, but she earns a little extra money by sewing. She wants to use it to help a black child go to school.

"This letter says she will pay a girl's way at Scotia Seminary. That's the school for black girls in Concord, North Carolina, where I studied. The school has asked me to choose someone to go. I choose you, Mary Jane."

"*Me?*" gasped Mary.

Miss Emma laughed. "You are my best pupil. School starts in a month, so you must hurry to get ready."

Suddenly all the McLeods were laughing and hugging Mary.

The good news spread quickly. Everyone was happy for Mary. Friends knitted stockings for her. The white storekeeper gave her new shoes. Women for whom her mother worked sent pretty cloth to make dresses.

At last the day came for Mary to leave. Many cabins and cotton fields were empty that morning. The McLeods' friends had all gone to the train station to see Mary off.

Mary had never been on a train before. As she sat down, she could hardly believe it. Bells rang. Wheels began to turn.

"Good-bye, Mary Jane," father called.

"Good luck, dear child," mother cried.

Smiling, an excited Mary waved to her family and her friends through the open window.

Evening had come before the train reached Concord. By then Mary's smile was gone. She missed home and her family. As she stepped from the train, she felt alone and lost.

"Are you Mary Jane McLeod?" asked a woman. "I am a teacher at Scotia. I have come to meet you."

Mary was surprised. "Why, they care enough to meet me!" she thought.

More surprises waited for her when she reached the school. It was a big, brick building, not at all like the tiny school in Mayesville. A girl Mary's age stood by the front door.

"I am Abbie Greeley, your roommate," she told Mary. "I have been waiting all day for you."

Abbie led the way up some stairs to their room. They were the first stairs that Mary had ever climbed. In the bright, cheerful room, she found she had a bed all to herself. At home she shared a bed with two sisters. Here she had her own desk and chair. She even had a wash-bowl all her own.

Mary looked at the bowl and thought of the tin tub at home. She remembered how her brothers and sisters all tried to wash their hands in the tub at the same time.

"Just wait until I tell them about my bowl," she thought. "Won't their mouths pop open!"

The idea made her smile.

"Oh, Mary, I'm so glad to see you smiling!" exclaimed Abbie. "You looked so sad when you came in the door."

"I was scared," Mary said.

"I felt the same way when I first came. Now I love it here. You will too." They heard a bell ring. "That means supper is ready," Abbie said. "We have the best food here. I'm getting fat."

Mary looked at thin Abbie and began to laugh.

Together the new friends went down the stairs.

Chapter 4

Busy Days

Abbie was right. Mary did love Scotia. Except for short visits home, she stayed there for seven years.

She studied hard to become a teacher. And she also worked hard, for Miss Chrissman's small earnings could not pay all of the school costs. Mary helped pay her way by doing extra work at school. During the summers she worked for white families nearby. Mary sent some of that money home to her father. He used it to buy another mule.

Mary wrote often to Miss Chrissman. The Colorado teacher sent her a Bible.

It was Mary's most treasured belonging.

One of the first things Mary learned at Scotia was that she could sing better than most girls. She had always liked to sing.

One day the music teacher told her: "You have a beautiful voice. So I shall give you special lessons. It is good for a teacher to be able to sing well."

One day Mary listened as a churchman told how the Mission Board sent people to Africa. These people started schools and did church work. They were called missionaries.

"Our fellow blacks in Africa are very much in need of help," the church-man had said.

"That is what I want to do," Mary told her Scotia teachers. She was almost ready to graduate. "I want to go to Africa and teach my people."

The teachers liked her plan.

"But you will need more training for that," they told her. "You must go to Moody Bible Institute in Chicago, Illinois. It is a school that trains missionaries."

Miss Chrissman liked Mary's plan too. She said she would help pay Mary's way at Moody.

So once again Mary entered a new school. Soon she was going with groups of Moody students into the poorest parts of Chicago. Their work was to teach about the Bible. They also tried to help the poor people lead happier lives.

Mary stayed at Moody for almost a year. She enjoyed her work. But when she finished, she learned that there were no openings for black missionaries in Africa. Tears filled her eyes.

"What will I do now?" she thought.

Mary decided to go home to Mayesville. She was grown up now—almost 20.

At that time few black girls had had as much schooling as she. Few white girls had studied for as long. Nobody could say to Mary now, "You can't read."

Home again, Mary picked cotton with her father. She worked with her mother, cooking and cleaning. She helped Miss Emma in the Mayesville school. And she wrote to the Mission Board, asking for a teaching job. The Board sent her to a school for black children in Augusta, Georgia.

The school was in a poor part of the city. It gave many boys and girls a chance to learn. In time they would be able to hold good jobs and lead good lives. But Mary saw hundreds of ragged, dirty children who were not in school. They ran wild in the streets, while their parents worked all day. She knew that something must be done for them.

"I would like to start a Sunday school for these children," she told the other teachers.

"They need help," the teachers agreed.

Mary went out into the streets. She stopped the first child she met.

"I am *Miss* Mary McLeod," she said, just as Miss Emma had once said to her. "I am starting a Sunday school class."

At first not many children wanted to come to her class. They knew nothing about going to school and were afraid. Mary was not discouraged. The boys and girls who came liked to sing, so Mary taught them new songs. She told them Bible stories. She was always smiling and gentle.

Soon word got around that Miss Mary's Sunday school was fun. More and more children came each week. Within a year 1,000 children were coming to the class!

Mary told them about God's love. She taught them how to keep themselves clean and how to behave. She made them want to go to school and learn to read and write. She opened a whole new way of life for those children.

The children taught Mary something too. They taught her that she did not need to go to Africa to help her people.

"Africans in America need teachers just as much as Africans in Africa," Mary thought. "Someday I will start my own school. It will be in a place where there is no other school for black children. I will try to do for them what Miss Emma did for me."

Chapter *5*

New Ways for Mary

After one year the Mission Board sent Mary to another school. This one was in Sumter, South Carolina, seven miles from Mayesville.

The first Sunday she was in Sumter, Mary went to church. She was asked to sing in the choir. A tall, pleasant young man named Albertus Bethune sang in the choir too. He and Mary became friends.

"Can you ride a bicycle?" Albertus asked Mary one Sunday.

"Goodness, no!" Mary laughed. "All I have ever ridden was our mule."

"I shall teach you to ride a bicycle," Albertus said in his quiet way.

He did teach her. Then he and Mary took long bicycle rides through the beautiful countryside. When spring came, they rode all the way to the McLeods' farm. Mary wanted him to meet her parents.

Mr. and Mrs. McLeod and Albertus liked one another at once. While the men were talking, Patsy drew Mary aside.

"Mary Jane, are you going to marry Albertus?" Mary's mother whispered.

Mary's eyes shone. "Just the minute he asks me, mama," she whispered back.

They were married in May of 1898.

Albertus Bethune worked in a store. Mary planned to go on with her teaching. Her plans were changed when little Albert McLeod Bethune was born. With a baby and a husband, Mary was busy at home.

The young family moved to Palatka, Florida. Albertus had gotten a new job, and Mary began to teach again. Palatka's school was small and run-down. Mary helped to build it up. Soon there were so many students the Mission Board had to send three more teachers. Mary was happy to see Palatka's school grow. But she had not forgotten her dream of starting her own school. It would be for little black girls, she had decided.

A young Palatka minister was interested in Mary's idea. One day he told her, "A railroad is being built down the east coast of Florida. Many black men have gone there to work. Their pay is small, and the families have a hard time.

"Daytona is the worst place. It is a rich and growing city. But the black people there live in houses no better than slave cabins. Many of the mothers have to work, and the children have no care. Something should be done to help those children."

Mary told Albertus what the minister had said. Then she told him, "I think Daytona is the place for me to start my school, Albertus."

Her husband shook his head. "You can't start a school, Mary. You have no money."

"I will find a way."

He shook his head again. "There is no way. But if you must, go to Daytona and see for yourself. I will keep on working here. If you stay, I will send you what money I can."

On a bright summer day in 1904, Mary packed a few clothes. With five-year-old Albert she took the train to Daytona, some 50 miles away. When she got there, she had $1.50 in her purse.

Chapter **6**

"The School"

The sky over Daytona was bright blue. A cool wind blew in from the nearby Atlantic Ocean. Mary and Albert walked up and down the streets and looked at everything.

In one part of town, there were fine, big houses. Many of them belonged to rich families from the North. They liked to live in warm, sunny Florida during the winter. There were great hotels and beautiful stores. There were flowers and tall oak and palm trees.

But the other part of Daytona was different. Here the railroad workers lived. Their tiny houses were unpainted and so rickety they seemed ready to fall down. Puddles of brown water stood in the muddy streets. Weeds grew everywhere. Mary stared at the crowds of ragged children playing in the weeds and mud.

"This is the place for my school," she thought. "These children need it. And Daytona has many rich men. Perhaps some of them will help me." She began to ask people if they knew of an empty house for rent.

"John Williams has a house on Palm Street," a man said.

Mr. Williams was one of the few black men in Daytona who owned property. He was sitting on the porch when Mary got to the empty house. It was dirty and ugly. Windowpanes were broken. The front

47

steps shook, and the roof leaked. But there were three small rooms downstairs and two more up. "I could live upstairs and use the downstairs for school," Mary thought.

"How much is the rent?" she asked Mr. Williams.

"Eleven dollars a month."

Mary held out her $1.50. "This is all I have," she said. "I will pay the rest soon."

Mr. Williams looked hard at Mary. Then he said, "You have an honest face. I will trust you." He took the money and left.

A happy Mary hugged little Albert. "We have our building!" she said. "Now we must get to work!"

When neighbor women heard that Mary was starting a school, they came with mops and brooms to help. They were poor. But, like Mary, they wanted their children to go to school.

They brought cots for Mary and Albert. They shared meals with them.

Neighbor men brought hammers, saws, and nails.

"We will patch your roof and mend the steps," they said. "We will fix the broken windows."

Mary went to the city dump. There she found a barrel, old boards, and large, wooden boxes. She took them home for furniture. Boards on boxes made benches. Other boxes made chairs and desks. Mary nailed a piece of pretty, red-flowered cloth around the barrel. That would be her own desk. The minister from the church down the street gave her a small bell.

"Every teacher needs a bell on her desk," he said.

The great hotels in Daytona threw

away many things that Mary could use. Behind the hotels she found cracked dishes, old pans, and lamps. She took them all home and cleaned them.

She went from door to door in the rich part of town. She explained to the people that she was going to start a school. They gave her a little money. Mary paid Mr. Williams the rent money.

"Now all we need are pupils," Mary told Albert. He had been helping too. He had kept the front porch swept clean.

Mary soon found five little girls whose mothers wanted them to go to school. The mothers worked for very little money. They could give Mary only 50¢ a week.

Mary decided to call her school "The Daytona Literary and Industrial School for Training Negro Girls."

"This is to be a new kind of school," she said. "The girls will be taught both lessons from books and homemaking. They will be taught how to earn a living. They will be trained in head, hand, and heart. Their heads will be trained to think, and their hands to work. And their hearts will learn to have faith."

Mary's name for her school was very long. Soon most people were just calling it "The School."

On the morning of October 4, 1904, Mary stood at the door of the house on Palm Street. She had not forgotten how Miss Emma had met her on that first day of school in Mayesville. Now, as each child came, Mary smiled and held out her hands.

"Come in, little girl," she said. "We have been expecting you. I hope you will be happy with us."

When the last child had come, Mary seated her pupils on the benches. There were five small girls and one small boy, Albert. She took her place behind the red-flowered desk. Then she tapped the bell. It gave a soft tinkle.

"School is now open," Mary told the children. "We will start by singing a wonderful church song. It tells how God's arms are always around us. I will sing first. Then you will know the words, and we will sing together."

In her beautiful voice she led off with "Leaning on the Everlasting Arms."

And so "The School" began.

Chapter 7

Hard Times,
Good Friends

The school grew—and grew.

There were 5 girls, then 10, then 20. Mary would not turn any child away. Neighbor women who could read came to help her teach.

Some of the pupils began to live at the school. Their mothers either worked at night or they worked out of town. Mary needed more beds, more food, more money—more of everything.

Mr. Williams, the owner of the house, gave her some old beds. A fisherman who lived next door brought her fish. Mary cooked the fish over a bonfire in the yard, for she had no stove. She and her pupils cooked elderberries over the fire too. They made ink from the juice. They used bits of burnt wood for pencils.

The fire outside worried Albert. "How will we get a stove, mama?" he asked.

"We must have faith that we will get one somehow," Mary said.

One day an old white woman came to the door. She asked Mary, "Will you read this letter from my son? I have lost my glasses."

Mary was glad to read it to her. Then the old lady saw the empty kitchen. "My son gave me a new stove," she said. "Would you want my old one?"

Mary wanted it very much!

Now that she had a stove, Mary baked sweet-potato pies. Every day she sold them to some railroad workers and earned a little money. But she needed much more money. Where could she get it? Then she had an idea.

Her little girls had become good singers. Perhaps people in the big hotels would pay to hear them sing. She asked a hotel owner. "Bring your girls," she was told.

Oh, what excitement there was in the school then! The children washed their dresses carefully. They practiced their songs. They fixed their hair.

On the big night 20 proud little girls marched into the hotel, singing. Their sweet voices filled the room where the rich guests sat.

The guests listened and clapped, and they wanted to hear more songs. After the singing Mary gave a talk about the school. The guests clapped again. One of them passed a basket, and people dropped

money into it. When they gave Mary the basket, it held $150!

Soon the children were singing in other hotels. They made many friends for the school among the people who spent their winters in Florida. One was Mr. John D. Rockefeller. Another very rich man was Mr. Henry Kaiser. Still another was Mr. James B. Gamble, whose company made soap.

And the school grew—and grew. In two years there were 100 girls. Some came from farms outside Daytona. Their parents paid for their schooling with chickens, eggs, and hams.

Mr. Williams owned a barn next door to the school. He rented it to Mary, so some of the girls could sleep there. But Mary knew the school must have more room.

"If I can buy some cheap land, I'll

find a way to build our own building," she said to herself.

Mary found some cheap land. It was a dump yard. Full of weeds and junk, it looked so dreadful that it was called "Hell's Hole." Yet, to Mary's eyes, it was beautiful. She saw it as it would look when planted with grass, flowers, and trees.

"How much money do you want for your land?" Mary asked the owner.

"I must get two hundred dollars," Mr. Kinsey said.

"How much will you take for now?"

"How much do you have?" he asked.

Mary showed him. She had five dollars. He looked at her hard, just as Mr. Williams had once done. Then, like Mr. Williams, he said, "Well, you've got an honest face. I guess you'll pay the rest."

Mary and her girls began to clean up Hell's Hole.

They had plenty of help. Mary had started an evening class for grown people. She taught the women how to keep their houses clean and neat. She showed them better ways to cook. She taught the men how to plant gardens, so they could grow their own food. She told them it was important to keep their houses painted and the weeds cut. She was doing the sort of missionary work she had learned at Moody. Now, when she went to Hell's Hole, everyone in her class went too.

The junk was pulled away. The weeds were cut. Then Mary took a painter to the spot. She told him to paint a sign pointing to the school.

He looked around at the bare earth.

"But where is this school?" he asked.

"Right here, where we are standing," Mary told him happily. "All I need to do is find the money to build it."

Chapter *8*

A Dream Come True

Finding so much money was not easy.

Mary wrote to friends of the school
and asked for help. She gave talks to
Daytona people. She went to kind Mr.
Gamble. At last she had enough money
to start to build a four-story, wooden
building.

When the sides were up and the roof
on, the pupils moved into the building.
The ground floor was still bare earth.
There was no glass in the windows. Some

of the walls were only rough boards with cracks, where the rain came in.

Mary had to find money to finish the school. She also had to find money to buy food and to pay the other teachers. It was a hard job. Yet she never lost faith that things would work out. She named the new building "Faith Hall."

One morning the kitchen shelves held only two cans of molasses, some rice, and beans. With her last few dollars, Mary started for the grocery store. A white-haired man in a big car stopped her.

"I heard your little girls sing at the hotel," he said. "May I see your school?"

In the school the old gentleman looked at the kitchen shelves. "Is that all the food you have?" he asked.

Then he saw the school's one worn-out sewing machine. "Is that the only sewing machine you have?"

His sharp blue eyes saw everything that was wrong. But he also saw how neat and clean the school was kept. He saw the polite, smiling children busy with their lessons. He saw that it was a happy place.

"This school is the most heartwarming thing I have seen in Florida," he said.

When he left, he handed Mary $200. "Buy the children some food," he told her. "I will be back."

He did come back—many times. He was Thomas H. White, a very rich man who made both automobiles and sewing machines. He had Faith Hall finished. He even put in bathrooms and electric lights. He sent a brand-new sewing machine. When the weather was cold, he came with his car loaded with blankets. If a child was sick, he came with a doctor. For the rest of his life, he was the best friend the school had. When he died, he left the school $79,000 in his will.

As soon as Faith Hall was finished, Mary put a sign over the front door. It said: ENTER TO LEARN. Over the same door, on the inside, she put the words: DEPART TO SERVE.

To go out into the world and serve others was what Mary had always tried to do. Now she wanted her girls to help others too. When they finished their schooling, she hoped many of them would find teaching jobs. Then they could train still more young people for useful work.

Mary's first high-school class graduated in 1915, when the school was eleven years old. By then Mary no longer did much teaching herself. She had to spend her time raising money. But she was lucky in finding wonderful black teachers who were willing to work for little pay.

They believed in what Mary was doing, and they wanted to help.

Not all of Mary's pupils would become teachers. Some girls would have to earn their livings in the few other fields then open to black women. For this reason, the girls were taught homemaking along with their other lessons. They learned to sew, cook, and clean. This would help them get good jobs in homes, hotels, and even hospitals. Without such training, they could get only the poorest jobs and the lowest pay.

These were very busy years for Mary. Albertus had come to Daytona, but he did not like it there. He went back to South Carolina to work. Albert went away to school. Mary's father died before he could visit Florida, but her mother came.

Mary showed Mrs. McLeod the large school building and the beautiful lawns.

She introduced her mother to the pupils.

Mrs. McLeod watched the girls busy with their lessons. Perhaps she thought of all the years when black people couldn't even read the Bible. Perhaps she thought of Eli Cooper's cotton scales and how poor black farmers had been cheated. Now it was different. She knew that these girls in Mary's school would have better lives than their parents had had. And the girls would teach other blacks so they would have better lives. The learning would go on and on.

"This is *real* freedom," she said. "I always knew you would do great things, Mary Jane."

"It was not me," Mary answered. "It was God who made this school. And you and papa and Miss Emma and Miss Chrissman. And all the good people who have been friends of the school. There have been so many friends willing to help. All they needed was someone to lead the way."

"And you were born to lead," her mother said softly.

Yet to lead was not always easy. One day a pupil, Anita Pinkney, became very sick. She needed an operation quickly. The nearest hospital for blacks was in another city. So Mary took the little girl to one for whites in Daytona.

"Negroes are not allowed inside this hospital," said the doctor.

"Please help her," Mary begged. "The child will die if you don't."

The doctor frowned. "You should not have brought her here," he said. Then he had Anita put on the back porch, behind the kitchen. It was a noisy spot, and it smelled of cooking. There he operated.

Anita did get well. But an angry Mary

went to many of the school's friends. She told them how the sick child had been treated.

"My people need a hospital," she said.

They helped her buy a small house near the school. Black people gave money and worked hard to make it a two-bed hospital. In time that little place became a fine, 26-bed hospital. Black girls were trained there to be nurses. Mary named it McLeod Hospital, for her parents.

Mary also helped blacks who worked in the forest camps around Daytona. The men's pay was so small that their families had to live almost like animals. Mary went to the camps and started classes. She showed women how to cook and sew. She taught children to read and write. She told the men that they must take an interest in government and vote.

Mary knew that voting was important.

It was the best way that blacks could fight for equal rights with whites. By voting for men who would help them, black people could get more schools and health care. They could win better jobs and fairer pay. They would be treated with respect.

But some whites did not want blacks to vote. Before one election, a group called the Ku Klux Klan tried to stop Mary. They told her they would burn down her school if she encouraged black people to vote.

"I will build it back," Mary answered.

She was frightened, but she did not let the men know it. Next day she led a group of her people to the voting place.

Although Mary was often tired and worried, she was never discouraged. And as the years passed, more and more people became interested in the school's work. They helped Mary to put up new buildings and to plan new classes.

In 1923 the school was almost 20 years old. That year Mary opened it to boys as well as girls. The boys came from Cookman, a boys' school in Jacksonville, Florida. By joining the two schools, boys and girls could have good training at less cost. Mary was still the head of the school. But now other people would raise the money for it.

"The School" became Bethune-Cookman Collegiate Institute. It taught every high-school subject, so its graduates would be ready for college. By now many young blacks wanted a college education. Times were changing, and more fields of skilled work were opening to them. Mary's dream of starting a school had come true in a bigger way than she had ever thought possible.

Chapter 9

A Long, Good Life

"It is time for you to stop working so hard. You should rest," friends told Mary when she was 50. Mary's husband had died in South Carolina. Her son was a grown man now.

Mary tried to slow down. But soon she was traveling all over the country, giving talks and holding meetings. She was doing in a bigger way what she had done in Daytona. She was fighting for the rights of her people.

"You are free human beings," she told them. "Now you must be *equal* citizens of your country."

Mary started the National Council of Negro Women, which grew in time to include 800,000 women. The organization did much to help black people.

Through that work Mary met men and women who were important in government. One day President Franklin D. Roosevelt invited her to visit the White House in Washington, D.C. Bad times had come to the country. Millions of people were without jobs. The president had set up the National Youth Administration to help the young. He asked Mary to serve as Director of Negro Affairs for the group. No black woman had ever before held such a high government post.

Mary traveled 3,500 miles throughout the country helping to train young people for jobs and finding jobs for them. Often she visited President Roosevelt to tell him about their needs.

"Not enough is being done to help black boys and girls," she said one day, shaking her finger at him.

She stopped in horror. Why, she was scolding the president as if he were one of her pupils!

"Oh, Mr. President, I'm so sorry!" Mary exclaimed. "You won't want to talk to me anymore."

The president laughed. "I am always glad to see you and talk to you, Mrs. Bethune," he said. "For you always come for others, never for yourself."

Then World War II started, and Mary was made an assistant director of the Women's Army Auxiliary Corps. Her work was to help young black women in the United States Army. She made sure they

had the same chance to be officers as white women.

Before the war was over, President Roosevelt died. Weeping, Mary went to see his wife. She and Mrs. Eleanor Roosevelt were good friends. Both were especially interested in helping the poor. Mrs. Roosevelt gave Mary the president's hand-carved walking cane, and Mary wept again.

Two weeks later a great meeting was held in San Francisco, California. It was the beginning of the United Nations. People from many countries were there. They hoped to plan a lasting peace for the world.

Mary Bethune was sent to the United Nations to speak for her race. She told about the needs of black people. She gave advice on what should be done for them.

By now Mary was one of the best-known and most-respected women in the United States. She had done a great deal of important work, and she was given many honors. One was the Spingarn Award. This was a gold medal from the National Association for the Advancement of Colored People. It was given each year "for the highest or noblest achievement by an American Negro."

But busy as she was, Mary never forgot her school. In 1941, it had become Bethune-Cookman College. Every chance she got, Mary went back to the school. Many visitors came there to see her, for she was well loved.

Mary was almost 80 in the spring of 1955. She could walk only with the help of President Roosevelt's hand-carved cane. Yet she walked across the school's 32 beautiful acres. Hell's Hole had become a garden of grass, flowers, and trees. There were 19 buildings now and 1,300 students. Many of the graduates of the school held important jobs. Hundreds were teachers.

As Mary walked, her thoughts often turned to the past. She remembered the cotton field and the five-mile road to school at Mayesville. It made her happy to realize how far her people had come since those days just after slavery. She knew that there was still much to be done. Yet slowly blacks and whites were becoming equal citizens.

Often that spring Mary remembered something else from long ago. She had been crossing the yard to Faith Hall before the grass was planted. A little girl skipped along beside her. The girl dropped behind and began to take wide steps. She was stepping carefully into Mary's footprints.

"Maude Ella, what are you doing?"

Mary asked. "Are you making fun of the way Mrs. Bethune walks?"

"No, Mrs. Bethune," the child had said. "I am walking in your footsteps."

Now, in these last days of her life, Mary asked herself, *"Have* I left footsteps that others can follow?" She hoped with all her heart that she had.

On a softly blue afternoon in May, Mary McLeod Bethune died. She was buried near the school she had built, with much love and many honors.

Today, all over America, there are young and old walking in her footsteps.